KV-031-834

YOU ARE HERE
The Best of Kevin Woodcock

Kevin Woodcock was born in Leicester in 1942. After studying at art college and working at a variety of jobs he became a full-time cartoonist in 1970, and currently contributes to magazines in the U.K. and Europe.

Previous books by Kevin Woodcock

The Jokes of Kevin Woodcock
City Rules O.K.

YOU ARE HERE
THE BEST OF
KEVIN WOODCOCK
Fontana/Collins

This collection first published
in 1987 by Fontana Paperbacks,
8 Grafton Street, London W1X 3LA

Copyright © Kevin Woodcock, 1987

Made and printed in Great Britain by
William Collins Sons & Co. Ltd, Glasgow

A number of these cartoons have been previously published, either in book form (*The Jokes of Kevin Woodcock*, Private Eye Cartoon Library 9, 1978; *City Rules O.K.*, Unwin Paperbacks, 1983) or in magazines (*Punch*; *Spectator*; *Private Eye*; *New Scientist*) and are reproduced here by kind permission of their publishers

Conditions of Sale
This book is sold subject to the condition that it shall not, by way of trade or otherwise, be lent, re-sold, hired out or otherwise circulated without the publisher's prior consent in any form of binding or cover other than that in which it is published and without a similar condition including this condition being imposed on the subsequent purchaser

love

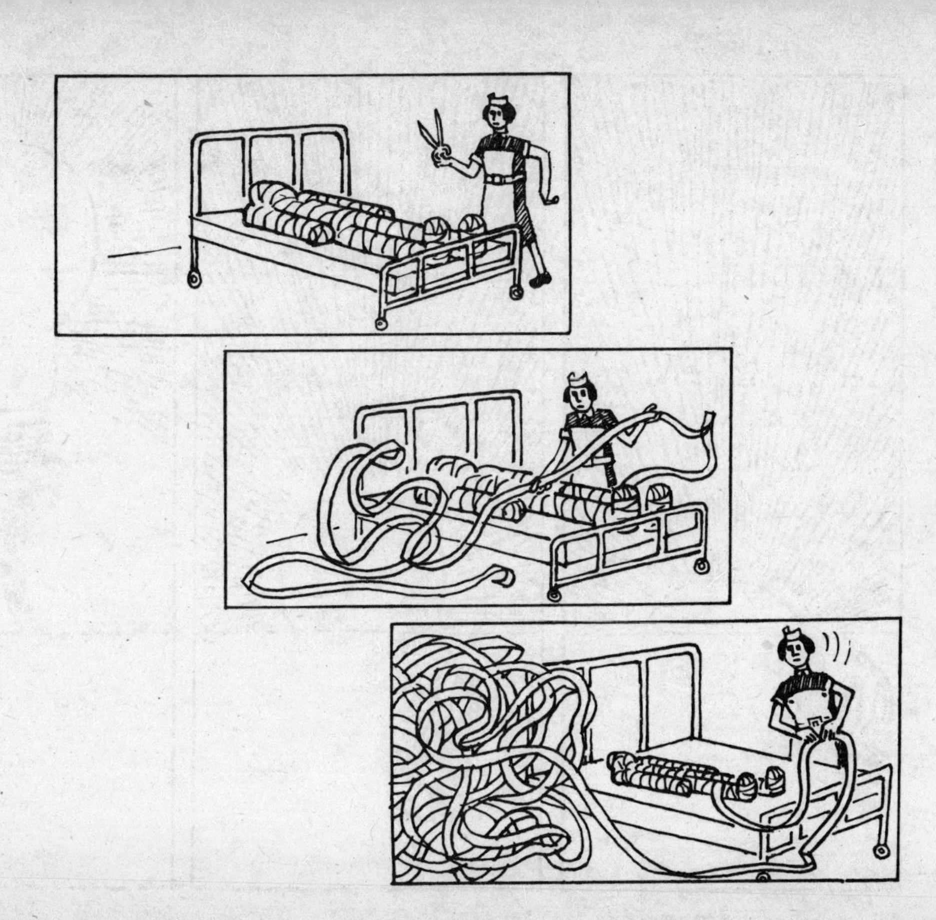

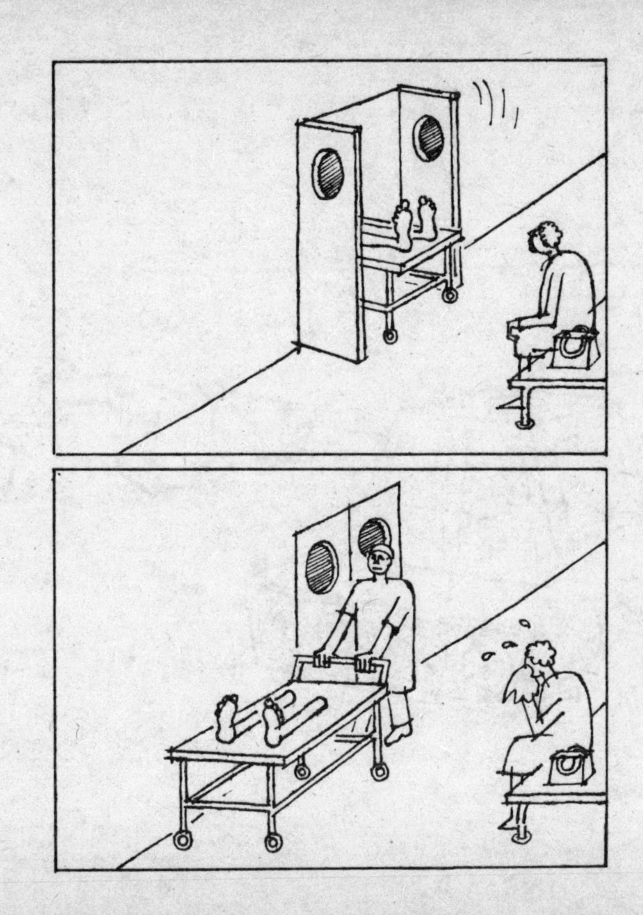

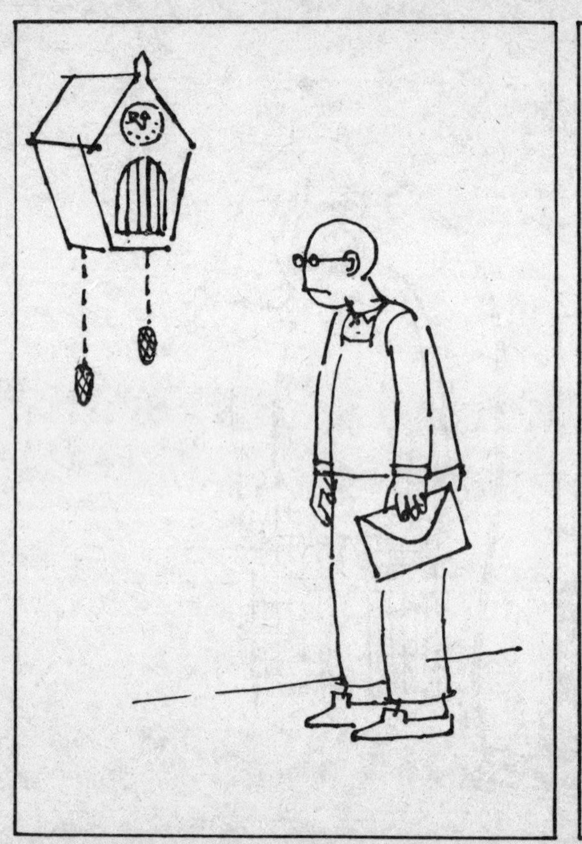

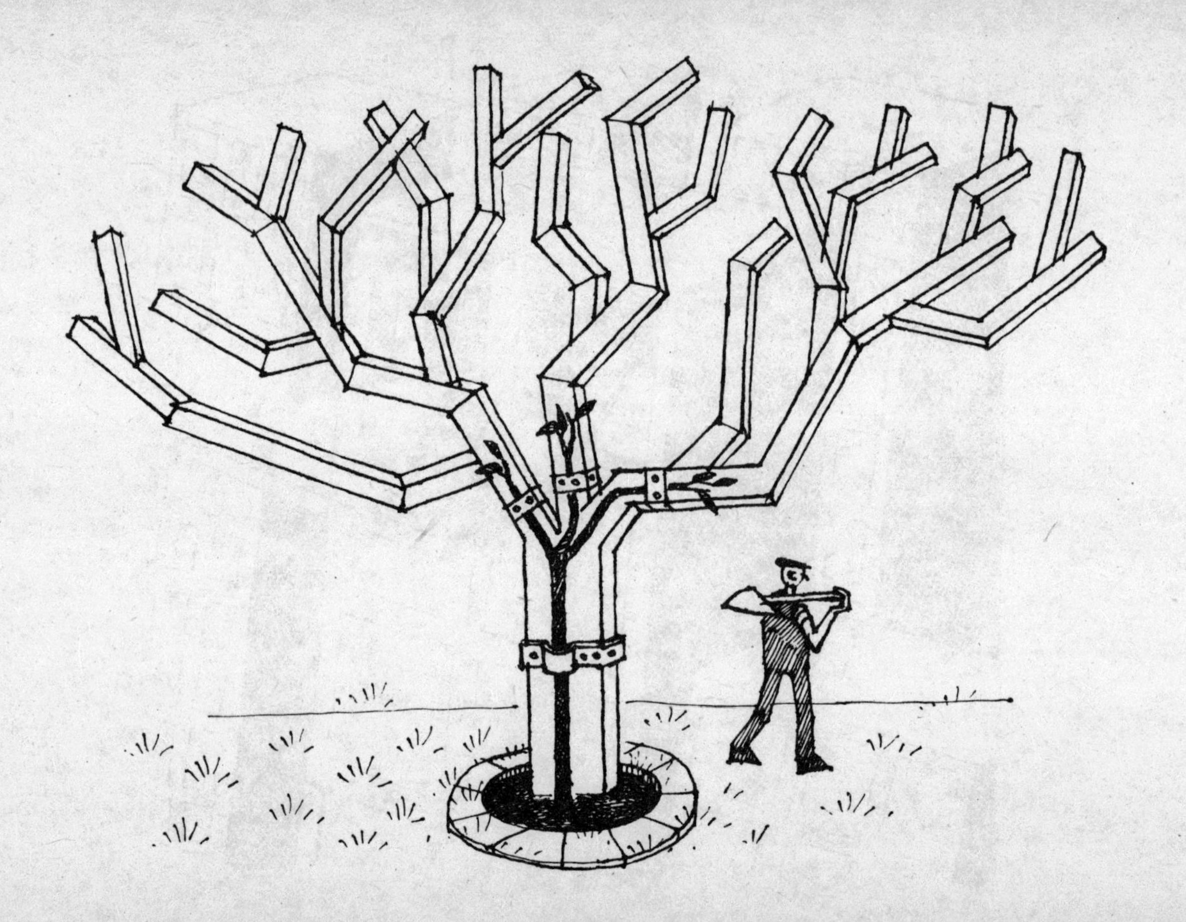

15.49

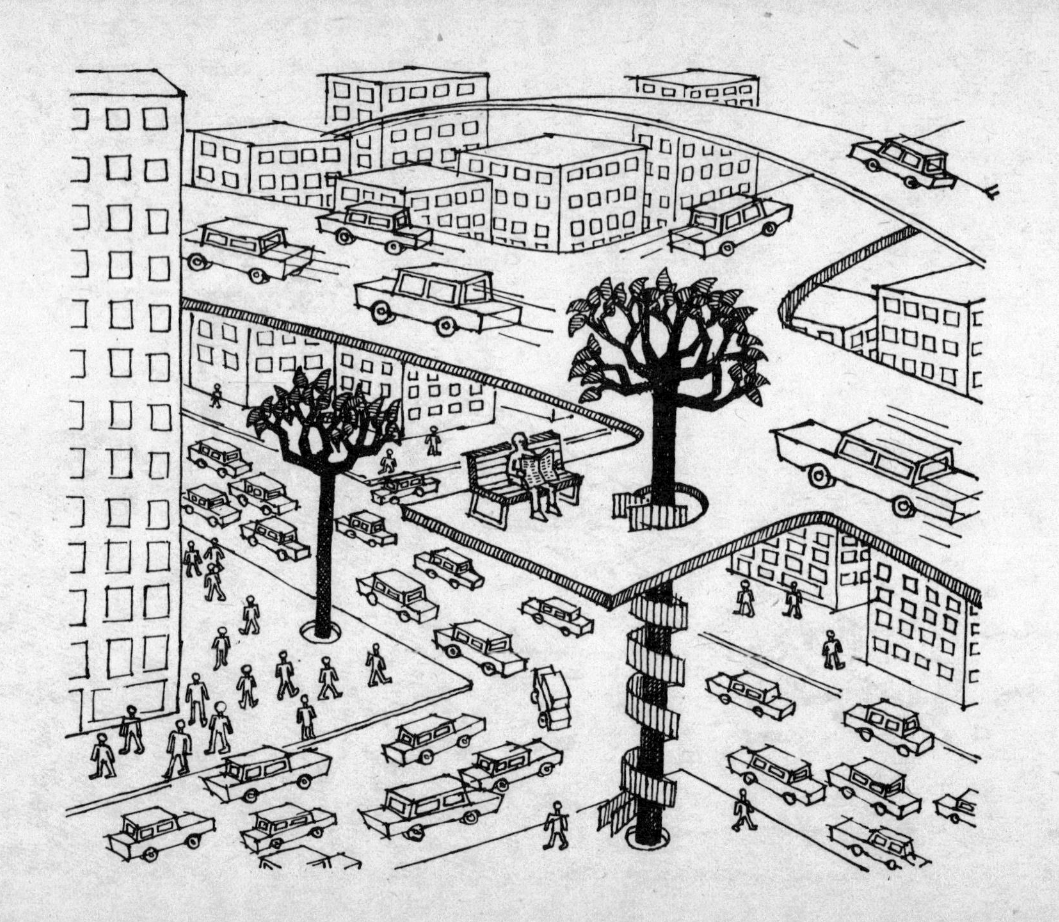

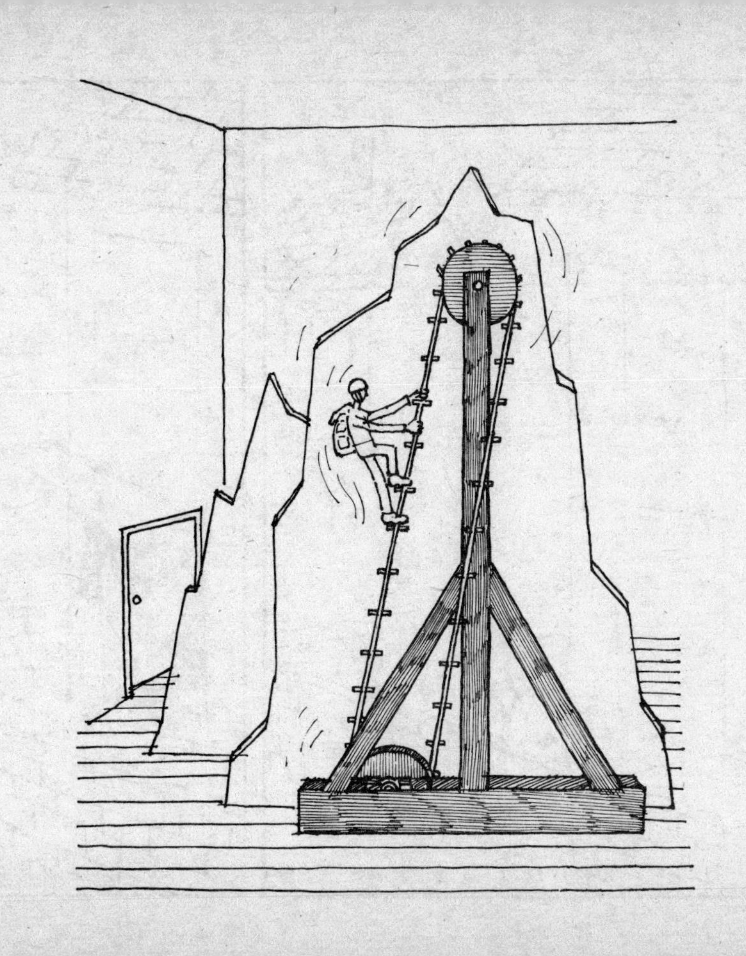

5

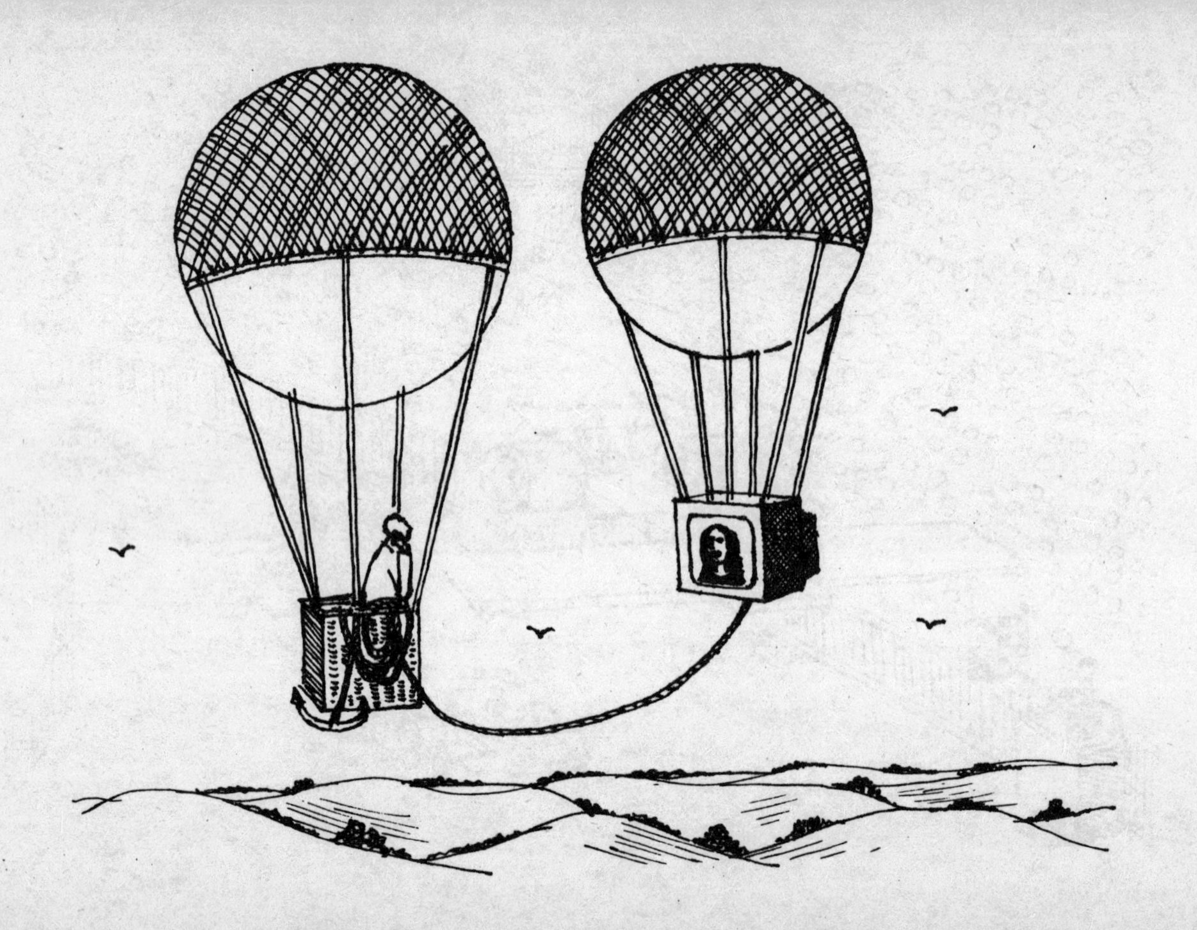

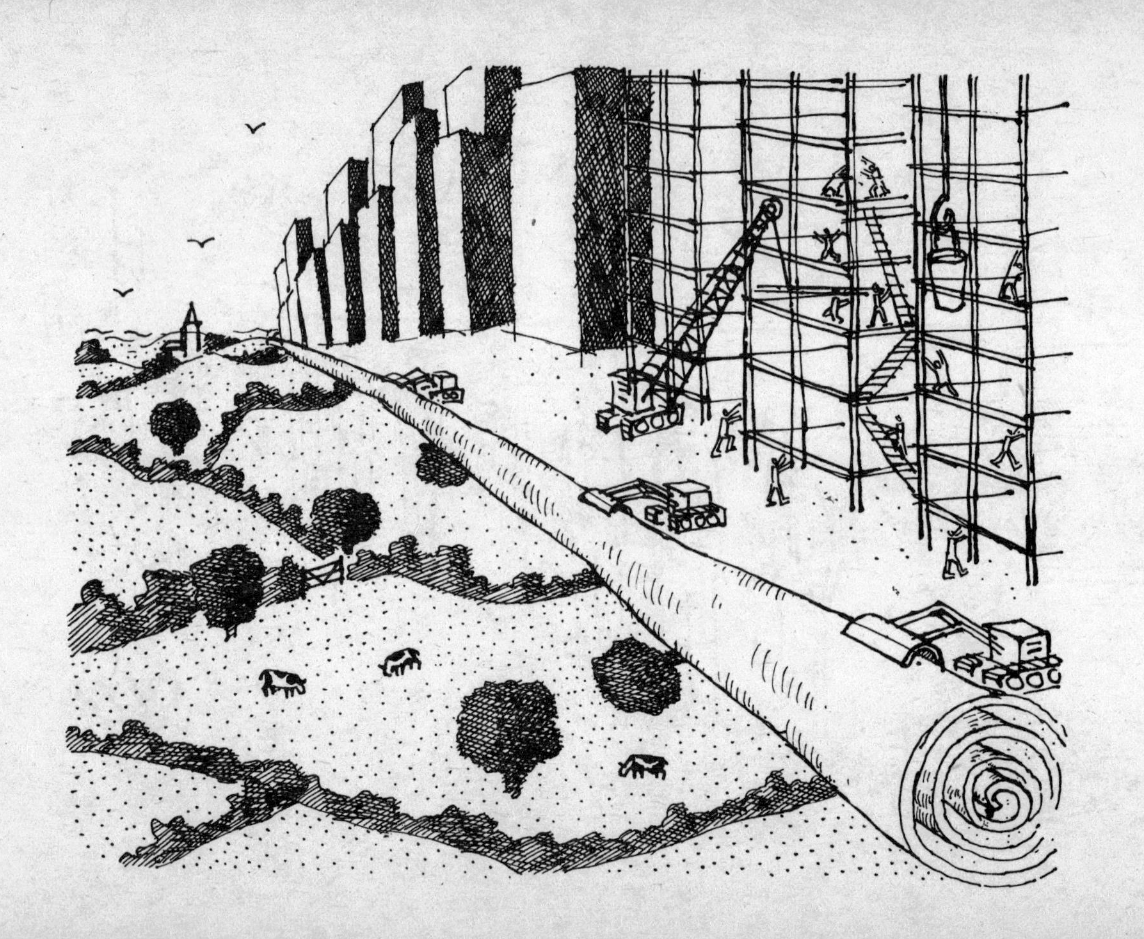

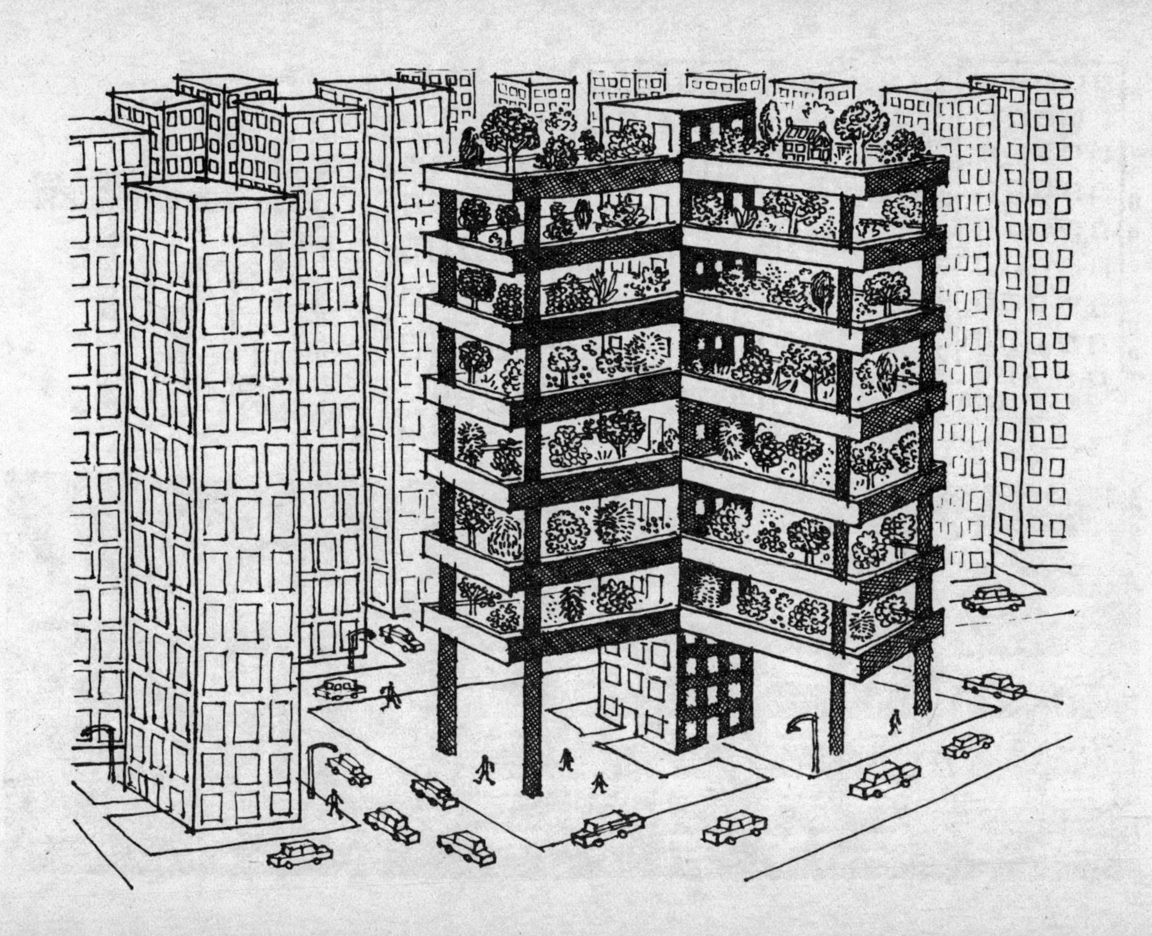